Numbers to 50
Contents

Teachers' notes	1	Marbles	20
Dotty dragonfly	5	Spelling check list	21
Dotty snail	6	Spelling practice – two and eight	22
0 to 50 number cards	7	Spelling practice – one to twelve	23
0 to 50 games	10	Spelling practice – teens	24
Parent's letter	13	Spelling practice – tens to fifty	25
Bean bags – 1	14	Penny games	26
Bean bags – 2	15	Number spiral	28
Darts – 1	16	Spiral games	29
Darts – 2	17	Sum hunting – 1	30
Boxes of eggs – 1	18	Sum hunting – 2	31
Boxes of eggs – 2	19	Tables square	32

Teachers' notes

Aim of this book
The aim of this book is to provide you with well-presented and mathematically valuable supplementary material which will link with your existing scheme of work for mathematics, and which children will also enjoy using. To help you make the best use of the activities, please read the notes which follow.

Printing
Although photocopying on to white paper may be the simplest way for you to copy the activities in this book, do consider other alternatives. Some pages benefit from copying directly on to card, while others look much more interesting when printed on coloured paper or card. If your school does not have the facilities to do this, you may be able to have copies made using a duplicator or printing machine at a larger primary school or secondary close to you, or perhaps at a teachers' centre.

To keep re-usable cards or worksheets in good condition, put them inside plastic wallets, laminate them, or cover them with sticky plastic. Even copies made on paper are surprisingly strong when covered.

Record-keeping and storage
We have not provided a separate system of record keeping for these activities, as most teachers prefer to add to their existing scheme of records. You could use the child's own maths writing book to make a note of activities used, when this would be helpful information to have.

Worksheets can usually be fastened into the child's book using a piece of sticky tape at the side, like an extra page in the book, as an obvious reminder of an activity completed.

Mathematical content
This book provides activities to help children with counting, reading and writing numbers up to 50, and using addition, subtraction, multiplication and division in context. Written work is linked to practical activity, and the children are given the opportunity to make up questions and problems for each other. Calculators can be used to solve or check problems.

Every activity needs introducing by the teacher if the children are to make the most of it. Sometimes, activities may be taken home to talk about with parents or other family members.

Although this book concentrates mostly on problems using numbers to 50, you will find that as children grow in confidence they can extend many of the activities to bigger numbers.

Notes on individual activities

Pages 5 and 6: Dotty dragonfly and Dotty snail
Dot-to-dots are a good way to practise recognising numbers in order, in this case from 0 to 45 and 0 to 33. Let the children try working backwards, for example joining the dots from 45 to 0.

Pages 7-9: 0 to 50 number cards

Print these pages on to card. Use different colours if you want to make more than one set of the number cards, to make it easier to sort them out. Cover the pages in clear sticky plastic before cutting them out to give the cards longer life. Make the wallet on page 9 to store them in as shown below.

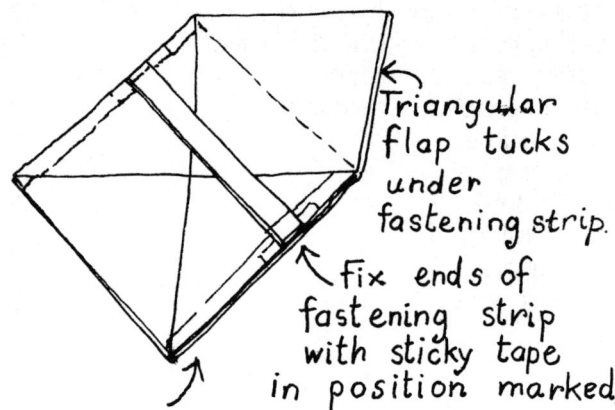

Triangular flap tucks under fastening strip.
Fix ends of fastening strip with sticky tape in position marked.
Fix sides with sticky tape.

You will probably think of several ways in which you can use the cards. There are workcards to use with them on pages 10-12.

The 0 to 50 number cards can also be used with the counting equipment (for example, the 'Parrot counting cards') in two other books in the *Essentials for Maths* series, *Numbers to 9* and *Numbers to 20*.

Pages 10-13: 0 to 50 games

Print pages 10, 11 and 12 on card, colour them in if you wish, and cut them in half along the dotted line. The set of six cards describes a group of progressively more difficult activities which can be played with, say, just the 0 to 30 cards at first, then extended to use larger numbers of cards as the children gain in confidence. Introduce each activity yourself, then leave the cards as a reminder for the group who are playing.

The children's progress will be much faster if you can involve older pupils, or parents, or other family members, in playing the games. Use the letter on page 13 to send home. Copy pages 10-12 on to paper, cut them in two and staple them together along the left-hand side to make a booklet to accompany the letter. A set of 0 to 50 cards (pages 7-9) should also be included.

Pages 14 and 15: Bean bags 1 and 2

These worksheets look at multiples of small numbers. They are most effective if the children have had an opportunity to play the game shown. Once a child has completed page 14 successfully, he or she can use copies of page 15, working with friends, to make up questions for each other. You may want to tell the children how many points to score for each bean bag, in order to practise a particular times table.

Pages 16 and 17: Darts 1 and 2

Like the worksheets on pages 14 and 15, these are most effective if the children also have an opportunity to play a game similar to the one shown (with a Velcro dartboard). Once a child has completed page 16 successfully, he or she can use copies of page 17 to make up problems for a friend.

Pages 18 and 19: Boxes of eggs 1 and 2

Page 18 looks at the six times table. Some children will find it helpful to have egg boxes available, with beads or cubes to represent eggs, to solve the problems practically.

Page 19 looks at division by six with remainders. Provide the children with counters or cubes to help them group in sixes, or encourage them to draw eggs in groups of six to help them to solve the problems and make up further questions for their friends.

Page 20: Marbles

This worksheet concentrates on the four times table, using the idea of scoring points for a game, as on pages 14-17. If you would like to provide the children with practice in a different times table, alter the number of points stated in the speech bubble, before copying the worksheet.

Pages 21-25: Spelling practice

Print page 21 on to card and cover it with clear sticky plastic to give it a longer life. The check list can seem overwhelming to children whose writing and spelling are still at an early stage; it is more effective to use it with children who already know the spellings for one to ten. One method of using it is for children to work in pairs, taking it in turns to take a card from the 0 to 50 pack, write that spelling down, and have it checked by their friend. The children can concentrate on just one section of the check list, by using just that range of number cards from which to choose.

Spelling practice is most effective in short, frequent sessions. Pages 22-25 provide practice for specific groups of numbers, and can each be used more than once if you wish.

Pages 26 and 27: Penny games

Print pages 26 and 27 back-to-back on card. Children seem to enjoy these activities most if they play them with real pennies. You could use plastic money, counters or beans, but it is not as much fun! Pennies also have the advantage that

● ESSENTIALS FOR MATHS: Numbers to 50

they can be stacked in piles, which encourages grouping in tens.

These activities are good ones for the children to take home to practice with family members, using their own pennies.

Pages 28 and 29: Number spiral

Print pages 28 and 29 back-to-back on card. You may want to print a few copies of page 29 on to paper, too, for the children to refer to when they are playing the first two games. The number spiral is also useful if enlarged to A3 size and mounted on card.

Any activities which you have used on a straight number line are likely to be useful on the number spiral. Number line activities help many children to build a mental picture of counting forwards and backwards, and improve their skills and speed at mental arithmetic. The activities described here concentrate on saying numbers out loud and do not require written work, although some children may want to write down what they find out when they play 'Spiral sums' or 'Jumping'.

There are more than ten sums which use + or – hidden on each page. Point out to the children that they may want to use a particular number more than once; they can draw loops which overlap.

Most children prefer to write down sums like 2 + 18 = 20, rather than using take-away ones, like 11 – 6 = 5. Encourage the children to use calculators to see that combinations other than straightforward adding are also true.

If the children want to make up a sum hunting puzzle, they will probably find it easiest to use centimetre squared paper. They should make up several sums, write the numbers for each sum across or down on the grid, then fill in the spaces with other numbers at random.

Pages 30 and 31: Sum hunting 1 and 2

These pages encourage children to look for links between groups of three numbers. Page 30 concentrates on combinations with a total of up to 20, and page 31 looks at more combinations of fives up to 50.

Pages 32: Tables square

Print this page on to card and cover it with clear sticky plastic to give it a longer life. It is most useful for children who have already spent time establishing their tables facts using activities like those printed earlier in this book, so that they can improve their speed and confidence. It is a useful activity to send home, or to use for five or ten minutes each day for a week or so.

National Curriculum: Mathematics

In addition to the relevant programmes of study in AT1, the following PoS from AT2 are relevant to the activities in this book:

Level 2
- knowing and using addition and subtraction facts up to 10
- reading, writing and ordering numbers to at least 100
- solving whole-number problems involving addition and subtraction
- comparing two numbers to find the difference

Level 3
- learning and using addition and subtraction facts to 20 (including zero)
- learning and using multiplication facts up to 5x5 and all those in the 2, 5, 10 multiplication tables
- solving problems involving multiplication or division of whole numbers or money
- understanding remainders in the context of calculation

Scottish 5–14 Curriculum: Mathematics

In addition to the content of the attainment outcome 'Problem solving and enquiry', the following attainment outcome and targets are relevant to the activities in this book:

Attainment outcome	Strand	Attainment targets	Level
Number, money and measurement	Range and type of number	Work with whole numbers up to 100 and then up to 1000 (count, order, read/write).	B
	Add and subtract	Add and subtract mentally for numbers 0 to 20; in some cases beyond 20.	B
	Multiply and divide	Multiply and divide mentally by 2,3,4,5,10 within the confines of these tables.	B
	Patterns and sequences	Work with patterns and sequences: – even and odd numbers – whole number sequences within 100.	B

◆ Name _____

Dotty dragonfly

◆ ESSENTIALS FOR MATHS: Numbers to 50

◆ Name ———

Dotty snail

◆ ESSENTIALS FOR MATHS: Numbers to 50

0 to 50 number cards

◆ Use this page with pages 8 and 9 to make a set of cards and a storage wallet.

			0
1	2	3	4
5	6	7	8
9	10	11	12
13	14	15	16
17	18	19	20

◆ ESSENTIALS FOR MATHS: Numbers to 50

0 to 50 number cards continued

21	22	23	24
25	26	27	28
29	30	31	32
33	34	35	36
37	38	39	40
41	42	43	44

0 to 50 number cards continued

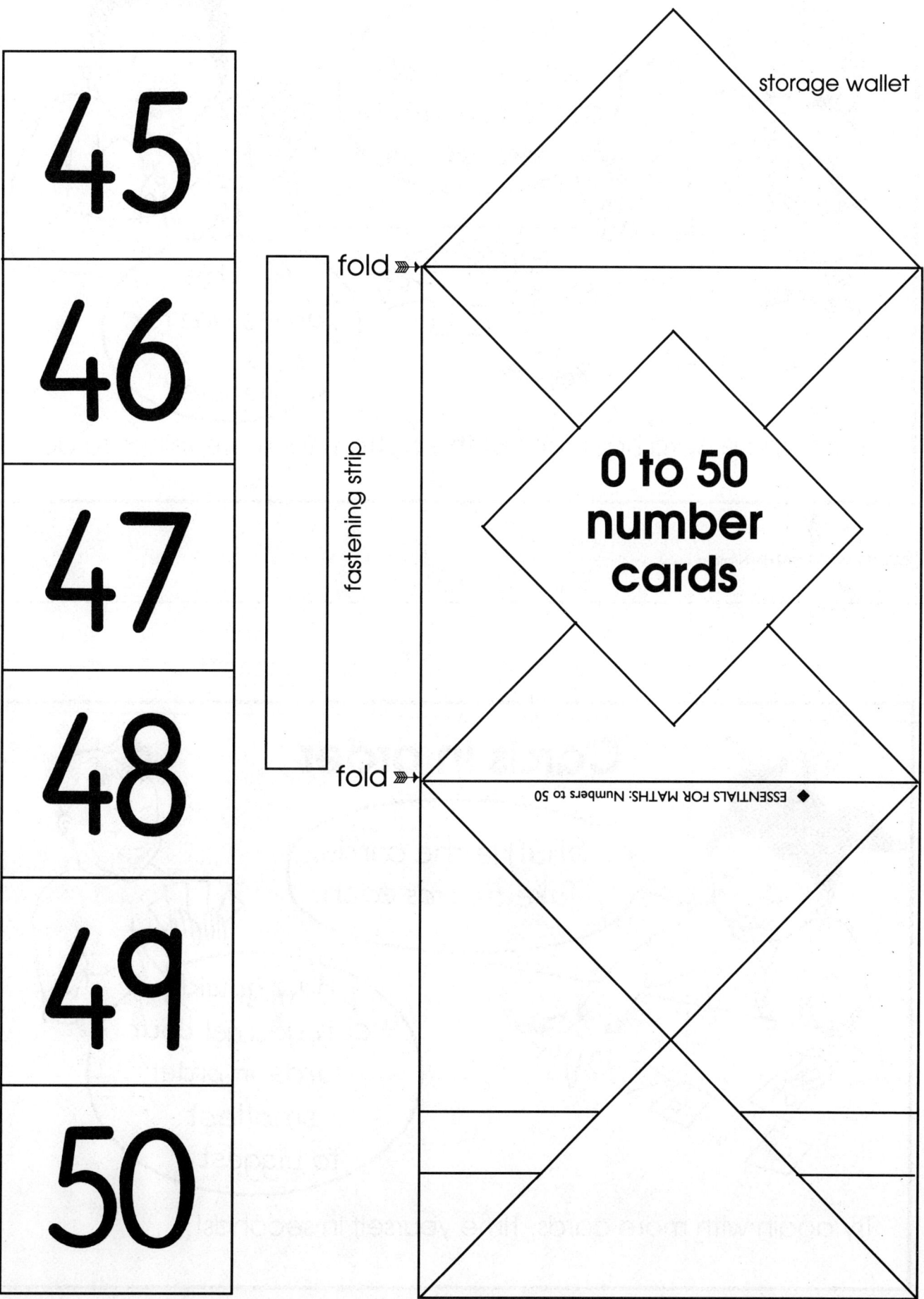

Each game card has ideas at the bottom for more things to do.

Try again with more cards. Time yourself in seconds!

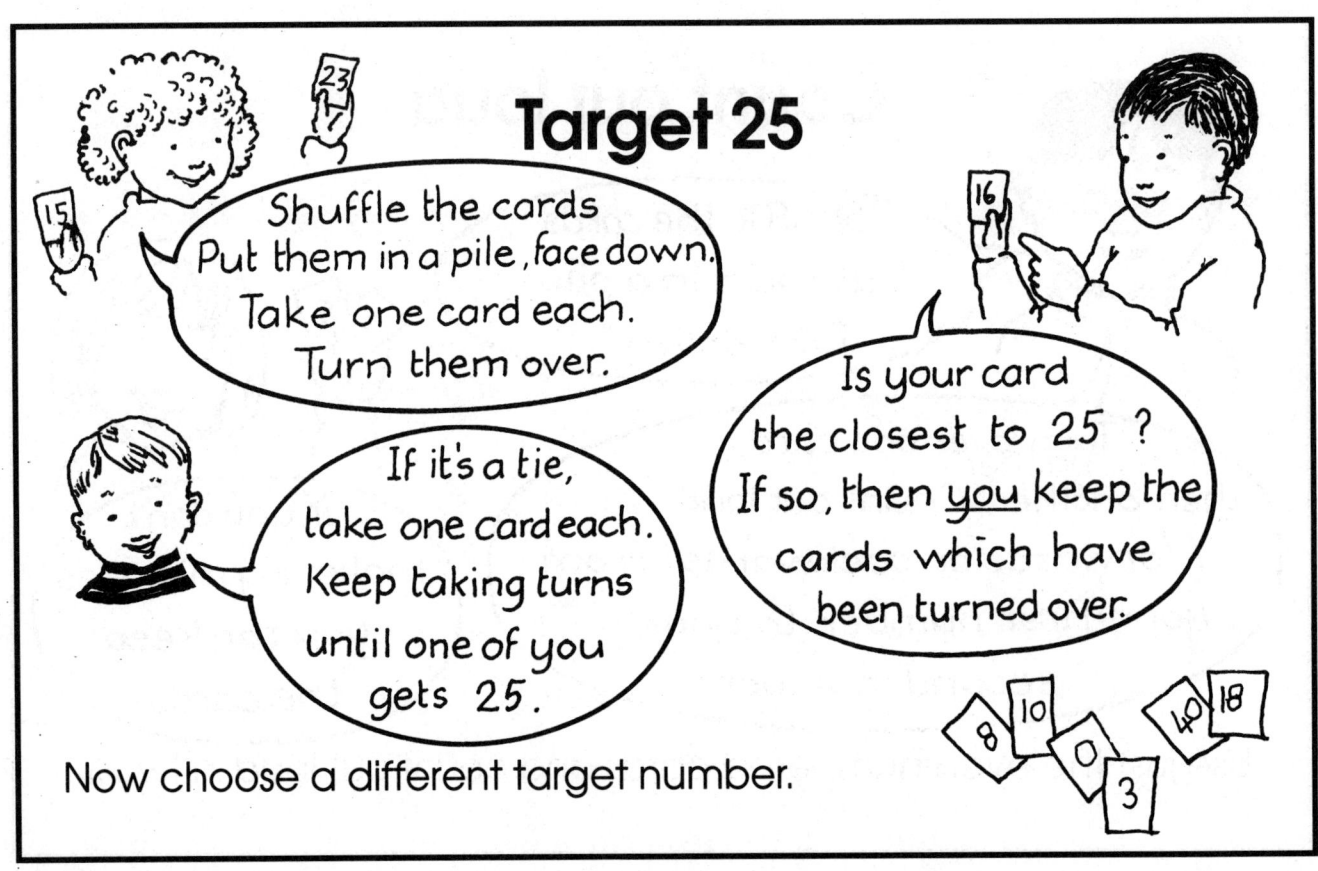

◆ Name _____

Darts – 2

Make up some problems. Give them to your friend to try.

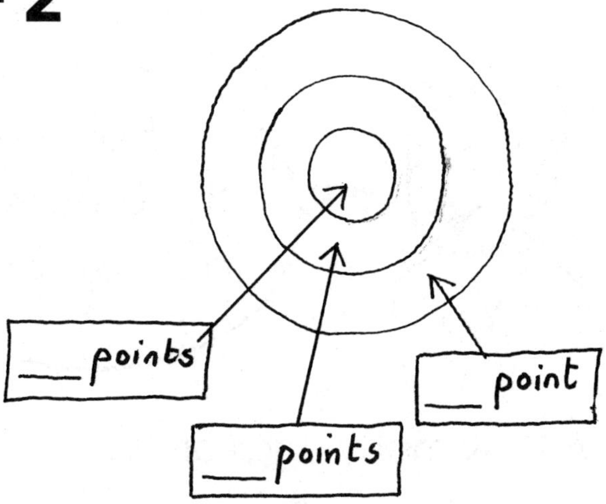

These problems are for

_____

___ points

___ point

___ points

◆ How many points did I score?

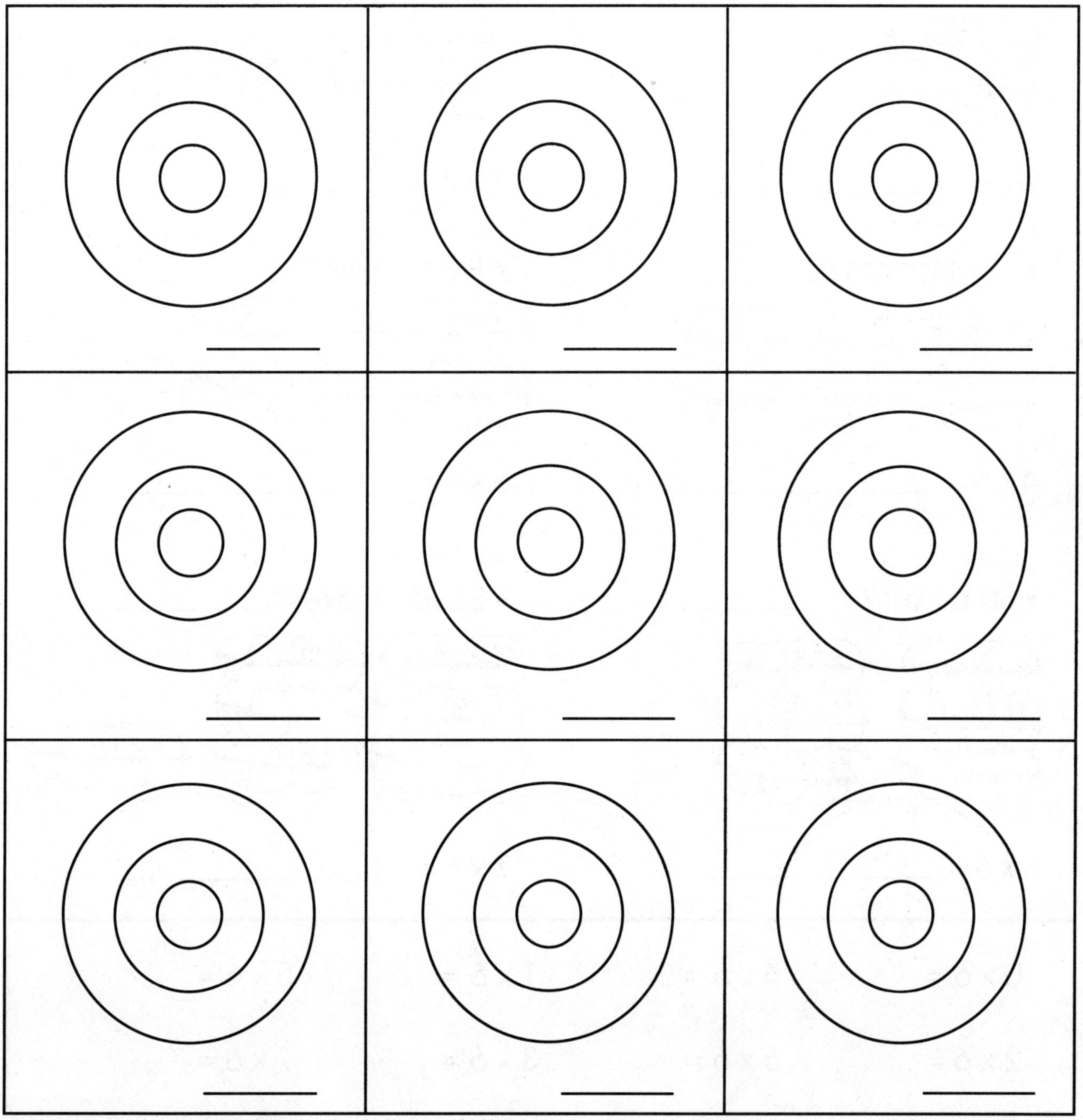

ESSENTIALS FOR MATHS: Numbers to 50   17

◆ Name _____

Boxes of eggs – 1

There are 6 eggs in a full box.

◆ How many eggs are in ...

• Two boxes? _____
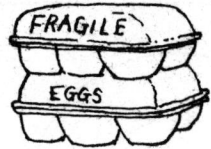
2 x 6 = _____

• Three boxes? _____
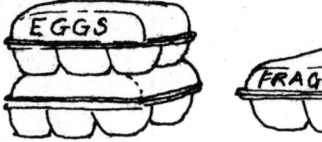
3 x 6 = _____

• Four boxes? _____
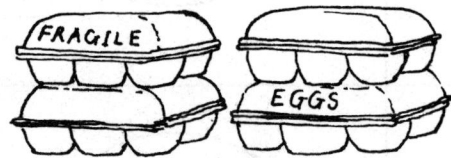
4 x 6 = _____

• Five boxes? _____
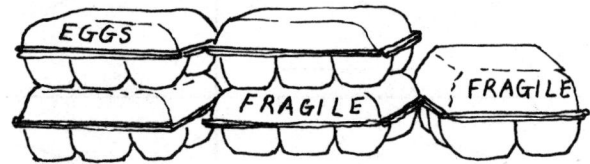
5 x 6 = _____

• Six boxes? _____

6 x 6 = _____

• Seven boxes? _____

7 x 6 = _____

0 x 6 =	4 x 6 =	1 x 6 =	5 x 6 =
2 x 6 =	6 x 6 =	3 x 6 =	7 x 6 =

◆ ESSENTIALS FOR MATHS: Numbers to 50

◆ Name _____

Boxes of eggs – 2

 I've got 14 eggs.

 They'll fill 2 boxes, with 2 eggs left over.

 22 eggs
How many boxes will they fill?
_____
How many left over?
_____

 10 eggs
How many boxes will they fill?
_____
How many left over?
_____

 24 eggs
How many boxes will they fill?
_____
How many left over?
_____

 37 eggs
How many boxes will they fill?
_____
How many left over?
_____

 33 eggs
How many boxes will they fill?
_____
How many left over?
_____

 Make up some 'Egg' questions for your friends.

Marbles

"I'll score 4 points for each marble I roll which stops on the star."

◆ How many points did I score?

Spelling check list

◆ Name _____

Don't try to learn all the spellings at once!

Concentrate on a few at a time.

0	none/nought
1	one
2	two
3	three
4	four
5	five
6	six
7	seven
8	eight
9	nine
10	ten

11	eleven
12	twelve
13	thirteen
14	fourteen
15	fifteen
16	sixteen
17	seventeen
18	eighteen
19	nineteen
20	twenty
21	twenty one
22	twenty two
23	twenty three
24	twenty four
25	twenty five
26	twenty six
27	twenty seven

28	twenty eight
29	twenty nine
30	thirty
31	thirty one
32	thirty two
33	thirty three
34	thirty four
35	thirty five
36	thirty six
37	thirty seven
38	thirty eight
39	thirty nine
40	forty

Be careful with 40! How is it different from 4?

41	forty one
42	forty two
43	forty three
44	forty four
45	forty five
46	forty six
47	forty seven
48	forty eight
49	forty nine
50	fifty

Use number cards to help you practise.

Choose a number, write it down, then check it.

◆ ESSENTIALS FOR MATHS: Numbers to 50

◆ Name ______________________

Spelling practice – two and eight

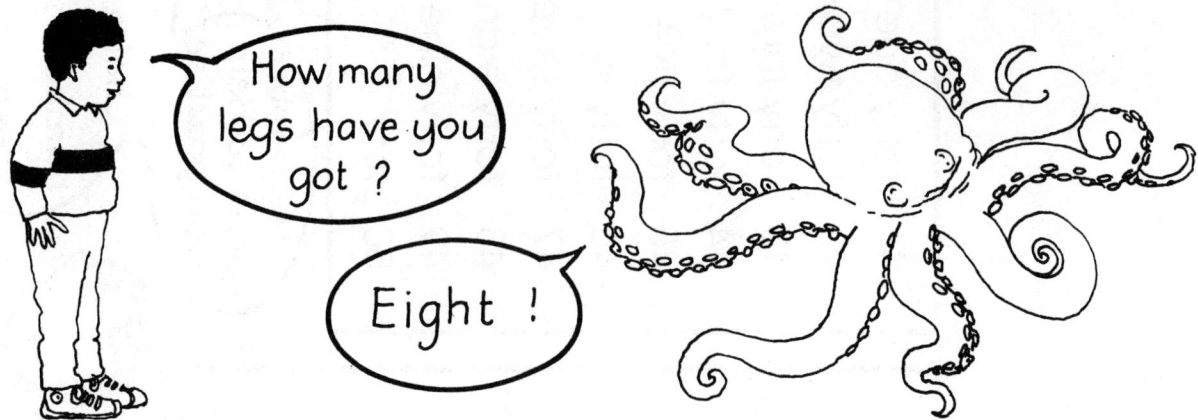

◆ How many legs have we got? Write eight or two in each box.

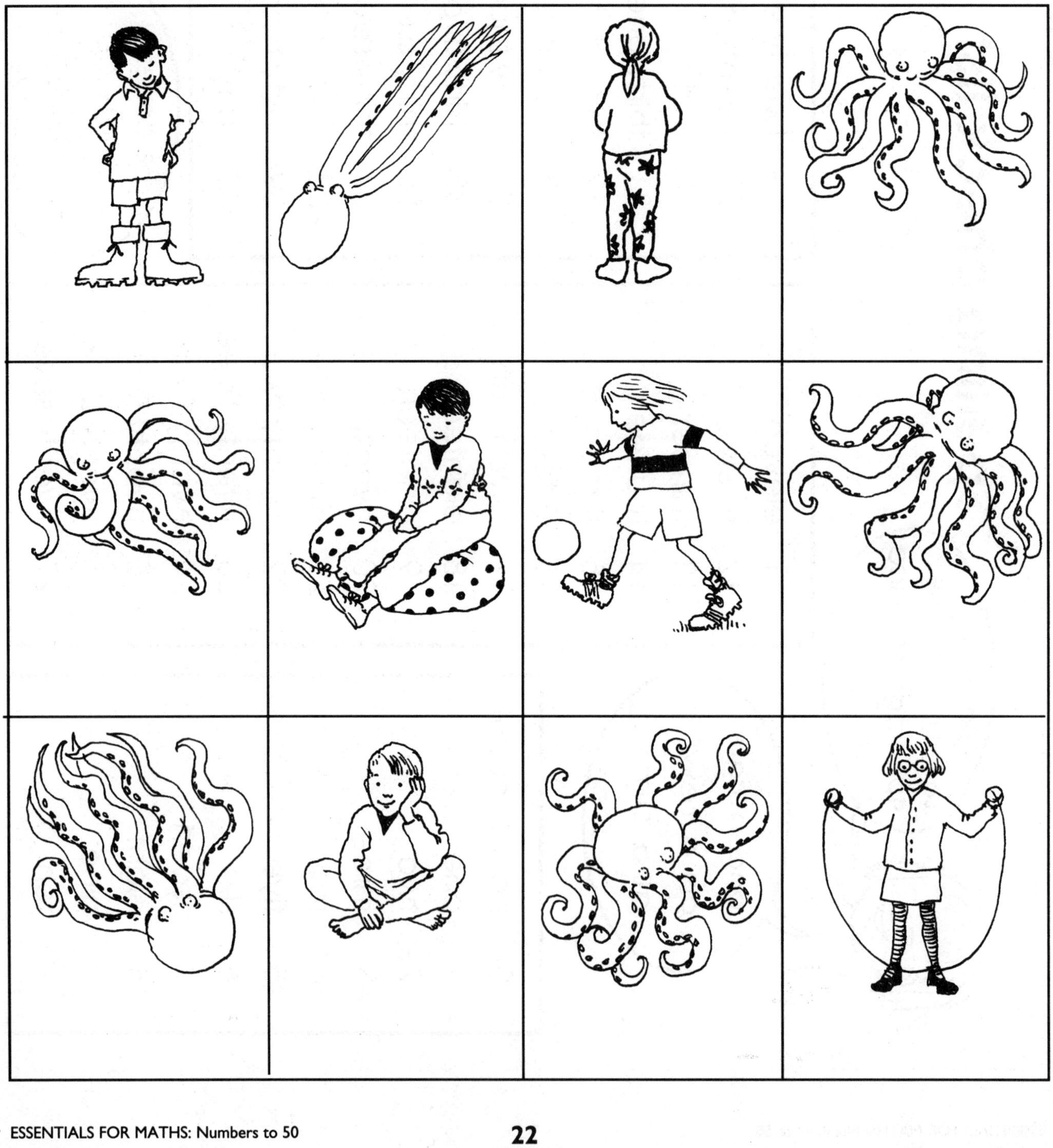

Spelling practice – one to twelve

◆ What time does each clock say?
Write one, two, three, four, five, six, seven, eight, nine, ten, eleven or twelve o'clock.

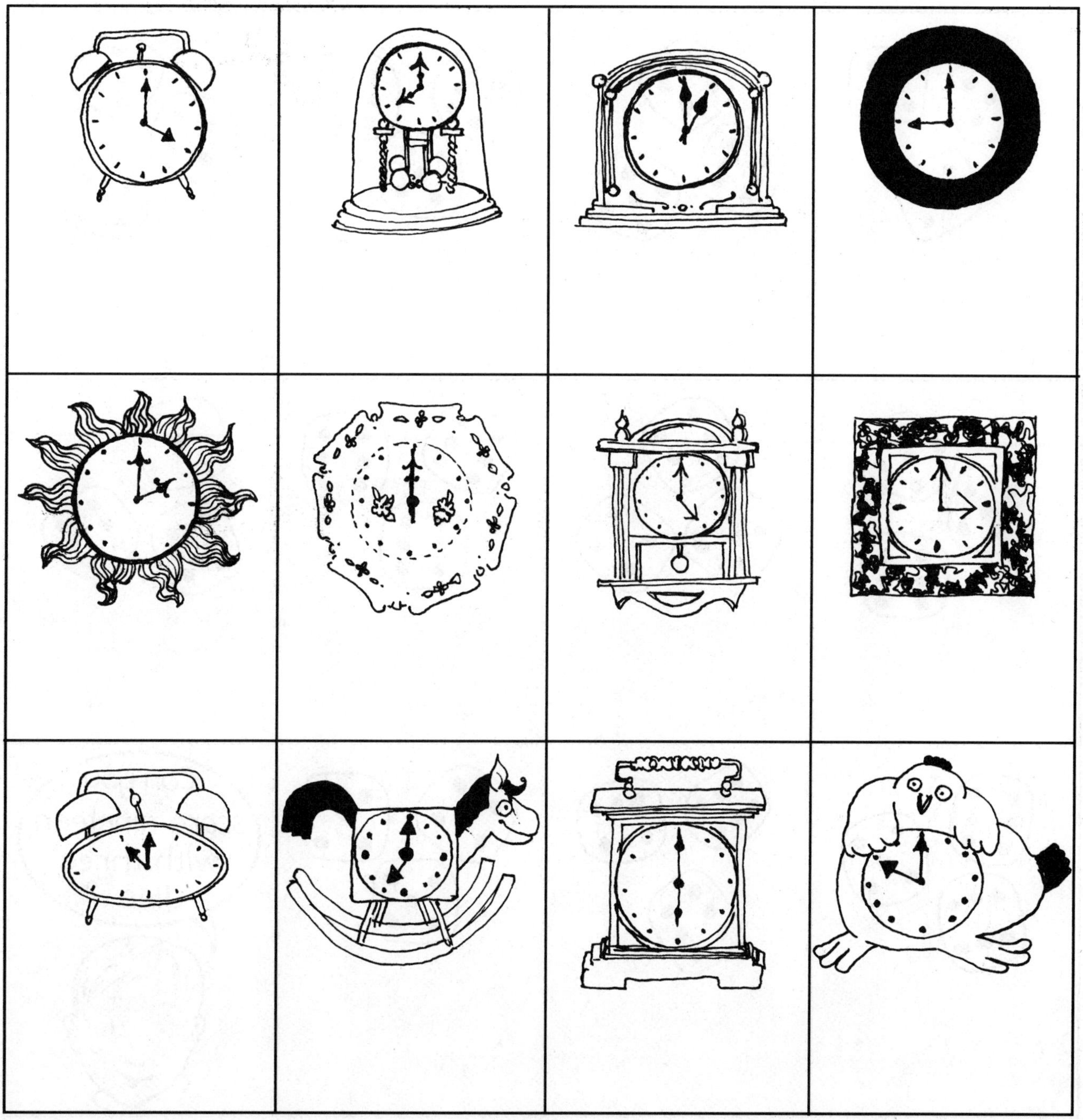

◆ **Name** ______________________

Spelling practice – teens

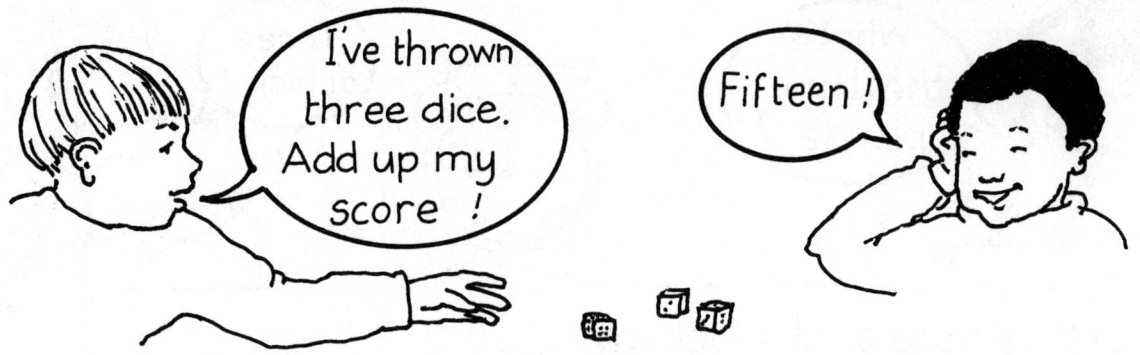

◆ What's my score? Add up the score in each box, and write thirteen, fourteen, fifteen, sixteen,seventeen, eighteen or nineteen.

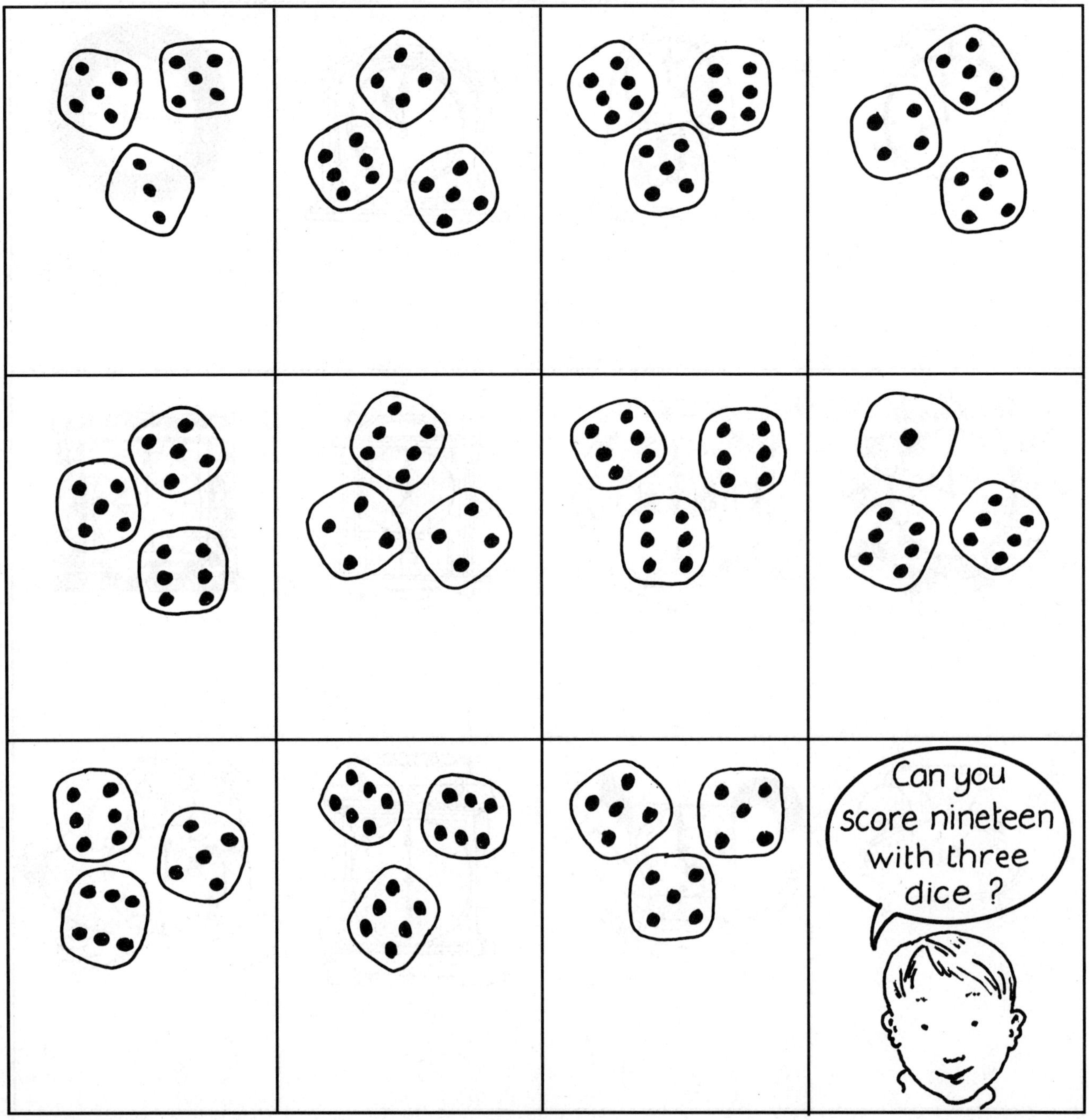

◆ Name _____

Spelling practice – tens to fifty

◆ How much money is in each box?
Write ten, twenty, thirty, forty or fifty pence.

ESSENTIALS FOR MATHS: Numbers to 50

Penny games

◆ To start with, use just 30 pennies for each activity.
Then use 40, then try with 50.

1 Guess and count

◆ Take a handful of pennies.
How many do you think you've got?

2 What's left?

◆ Take a handful of pennies.
Count how many you've got.

We're using 40 pennies. I've got 26!

Can you work out how many are left in the bowl without counting them?

3 Groups

◆ Choose a number: 2, 3, 4, 5 or 6.
Suppose you chose 4. Put the pennies in groups of 4.

I'm using 30 pennies.

How many groups can you make?

How many pennies are left over?

◆ Take it in turns to choose how many pennies to start with.
◆ Can you work out, in your head, how many groups you will make? Check with the pennies.

Number spiral

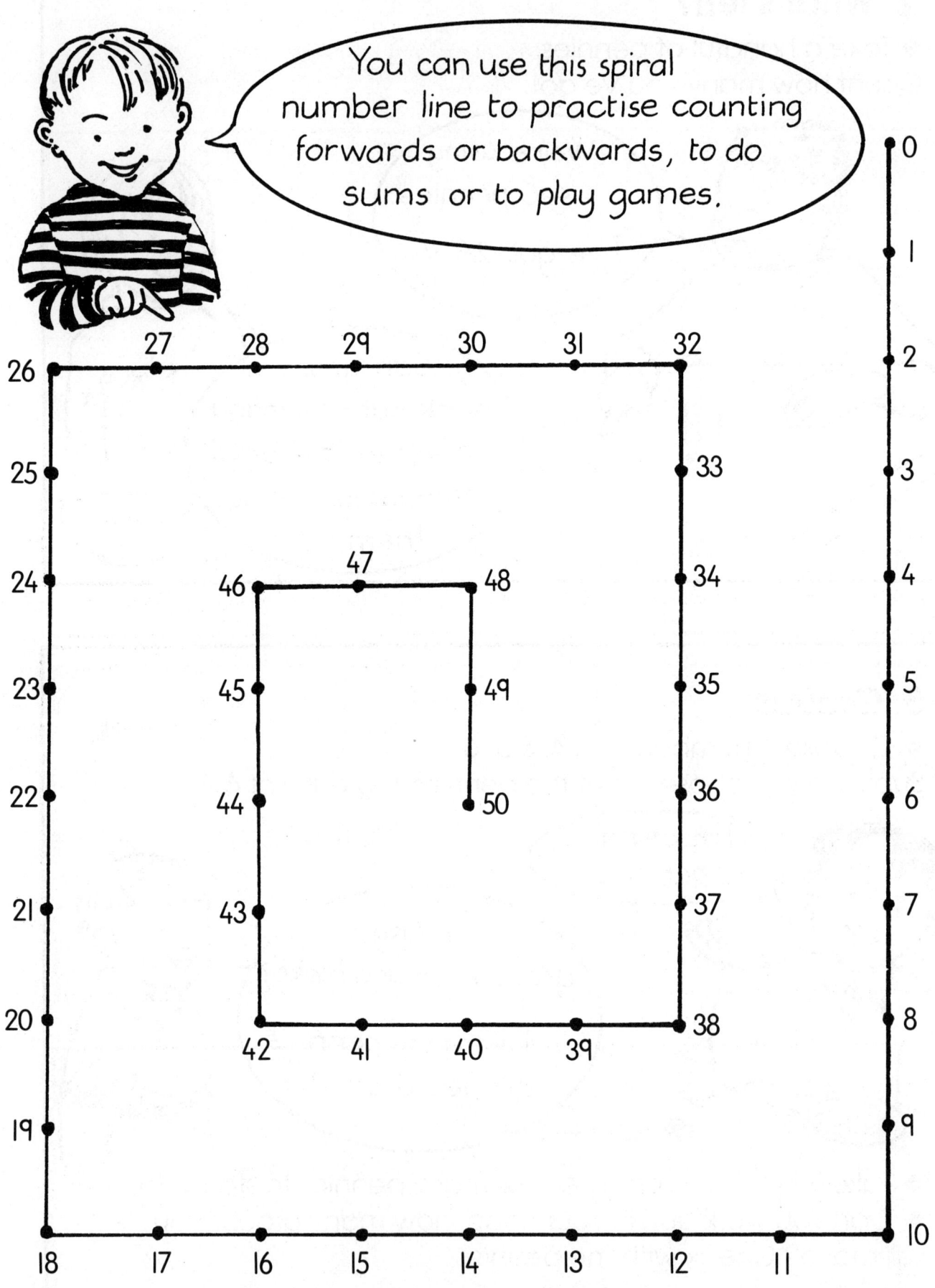

You can use this spiral number line to practise counting forwards or backwards, to do sums or to play games.

Spiral games

◆ You will need a 0 to 50 number spiral or a number line to do these activities.

Race to 50

Use a dice and a counter. Throw the dice and move that many places along the line. How quickly can you get to 50?

Missing numbers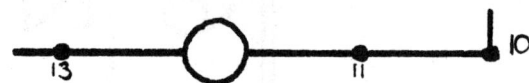

Use six counters to cover over six numbers on the spiral. Ask your friend to tell you what the missing numbers are! Then shut your eyes while your friend covers some numbers for you to guess.

Spiral sums

"I'm doing sums on the spiral. To do 27 + 6, I start at 27 and then jump on six steps."

"Did you get 33? You can check with a calculator."

Take it in turns with a friend, to make up sums for each other.

Jumping

"Start at 0. Jump three places at a time. You will land on 3, then 6, then 9, then..?"

"Can you get exactly to 50? What happens if you jump five each time?"

◆ ESSENTIALS FOR MATHS: Numbers to 50

◆ Name _____

Sum hunting–1

- Can you find three numbers in a row which make a sum?
- Draw a loop round your three numbers.
- Write your sum at the side.

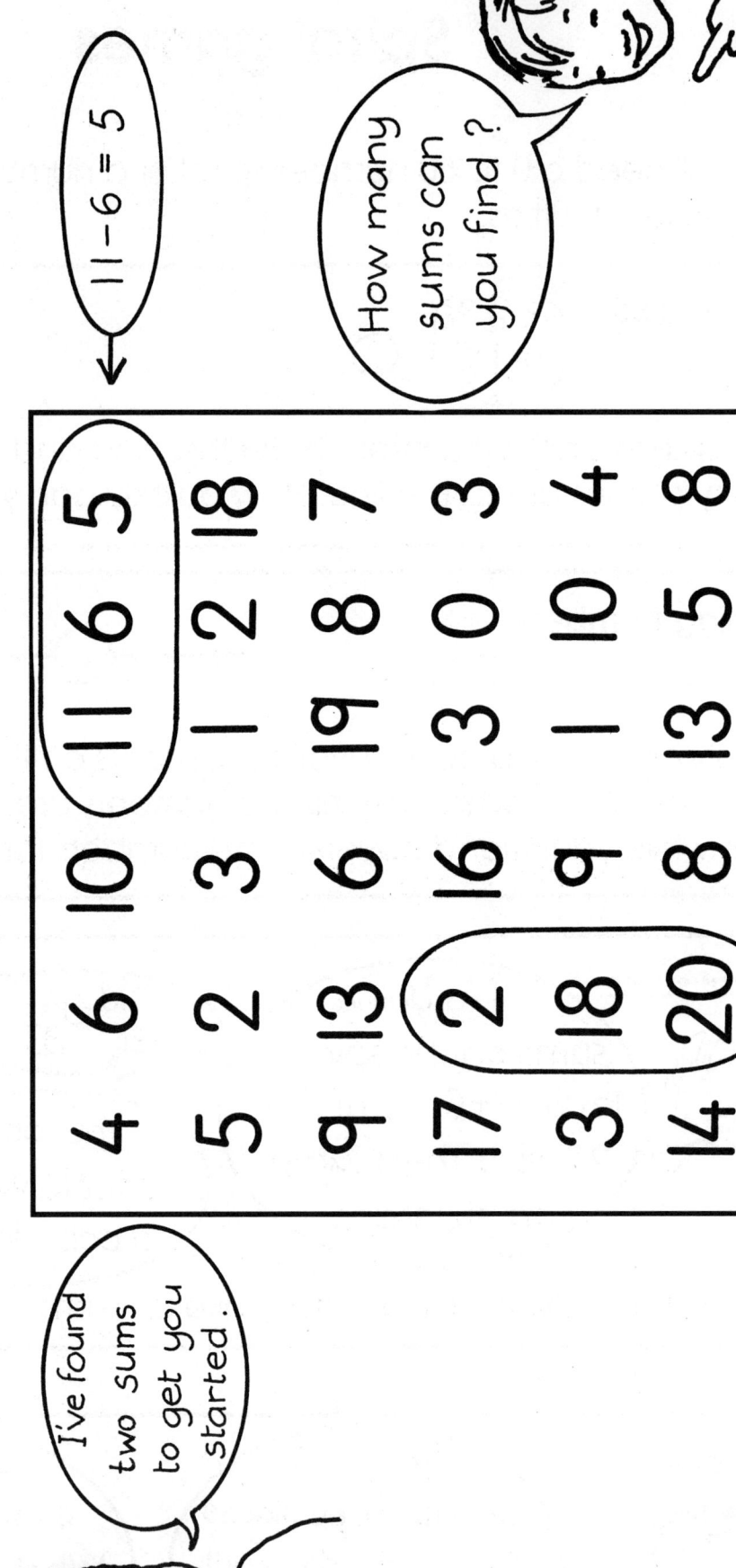

How many sums can you find?

11 − 6 = 5

4	6	10	11	6	5
5	2	3	1	2	18
9	13	6	19	8	7
17	2	16	3	0	3
3	18	9	1	10	4
14	20	8	13	5	8

I've found two sums to get you started.

2 + 18 = 20

◆ ESSENTIALS FOR MATHS: Numbers to 50

◆ Name

Sum hunting – 2

◆ Find three numbers in a row which make a sum. Use + or –.

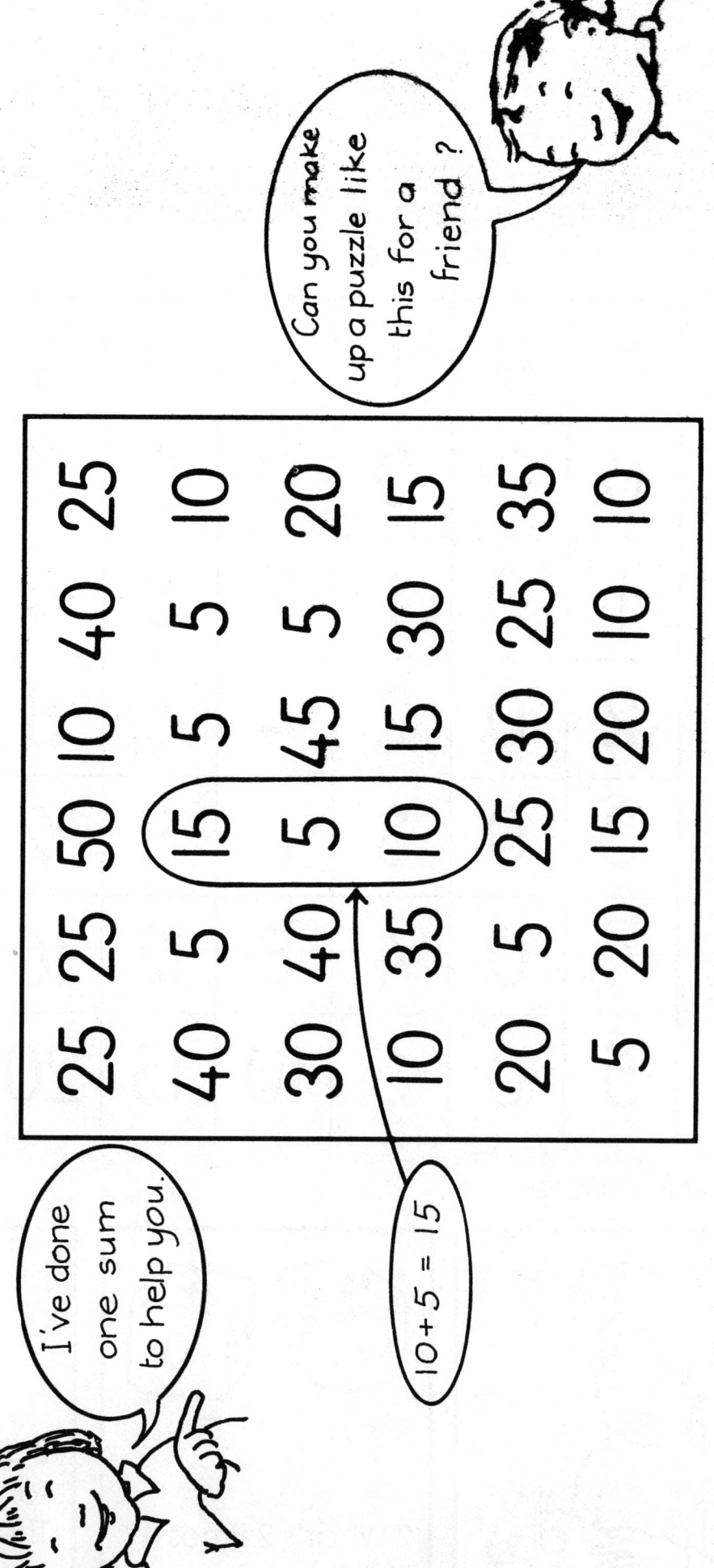

25	25	50	10	40	25
40	5	15	5	5	10
30	40	5	45	5	20
10	35	10	15	30	15
20	5	25	30	25	35
5	20	15	20	10	10

I've done one sum to help you.

10 + 5 = 15

Can you make up a puzzle like this for a friend?

ESSENTIALS FOR MATHS: Numbers to 50

Tables square

◆ Use this tables square to practise with a friend. You will need two 0 to 5 dice.

×	0	1	2	3	4	5
0	0	0	0	0	0	0
1	0	1	2	3	4	5
2	0	2	4	6	8	10
3	0	3	6	9	12	15
4	0	4	8	12	16	20
5	0	5	10	15	20	25

◆ How to practise:

1 Throw the dice.

2 What's 2 times 4? Eight!

3 Check on the tables square. Then it's your turn to throw the dice.